Happy New Year!

By Becky Cheston

Scott Foresman
is an imprint of

Glenview, Illinois • Boston, Massachusetts • Chandler, Arizona •
Upper Saddle River, New Jersey

Photographs

Every effort has been made to secure permission and provide appropriate credit for photographic material. The publisher deeply regrets any omission and pledges to correct errors called to its attention in subsequent editions.

Unless otherwise acknowledged, all photographs are the property of Pearson Education, Inc.

Photo locators denoted as follows: Top (T), Center (C), Bottom (B), Left (L), Right (R), Background (Bkgd)

Opener: PureStock/Jupiter Images; **1** ©David Zanzinger/Alamy Images; **3** ©David Zanzinger/Alamy Images; **4** The Green Bay News-Chronicle, ©Boyd Fellows/©AP Photo; **5** ©Design Pics Inc./Alamy; **6** ©Steve Vidler/PhotoLibrary Group, Inc.; **7** ©Israel Talby/ Israel images/Alamy; **8** PureStock/Jupiter Images.

ISBN 13: 978-0-328-46395-4
ISBN 10:   0-328-46395-7

7 8 9 10 11 V010 17 16 15 14 13

Americans celebrate the New Year
in different ways.
Some people march in a parade.

Some people swim in the ocean.
They hope for a clean, fresh new year.

Some people sing for others.

They wish everyone a happy new year.

Some people watch a Dragon Dance.
They hope for a lucky new year.

Some people eat honey.

They hope for a sweet new year.

There are many ways to celebrate the New Year.

How do you celebrate?